WHO MOVED
MY PULPIT?

WHO MOVED
MY PEW?

Victoria L. Burse

Copyright © 2020 by Victoria L. Burse. All rights reserved. No part of this book may be used or reproduced in any manner whatsoever without written
permission, except in the case of brief quotations embodied in critical articles or reviews.

All Bible References are from the NKJ Version unless otherwise noted, and all Websites and other links are referenced in the Bibliography and Reference section at the end of the book.

Published by the ARC

Riverdale, GA

ISBN: 978-1-7358104-0-9

TABLE OF CONTENTS

Introduction: Who Moved My Pulpit? Who Moved My Pew? 5

Part One: Who Moved My Pulpit? 9
- BE RELEVANT 10
- EMBRACE TECHNOLOGY 14
- RETEACH AND RELEASE 21
- AUTOMATE FINANCIAL PROCESSES 27
  - From your website 27
  - Mobile Apps 29
  - Giving Apps 30
  - Financial Transparency 32
- RENEW YOUR FOCUS ON OUTREACH 34
  - Sharing Information and Resources 34
  - Collaboration 36
  - Connecting 37

Part Two: Who Moved My Pew? 40
- WORSHIP 45
- TEACHING 46
- PRAYER AND PRACTICE OF SPIRITUAL GIFTS 47
- COMMUNION: THE LORD'S SUPPER 49
- BAPTISM 52
- EVANGELISM AND FELLOWSHIP 54
- IT'S TIME TO GO YE! 57

ABOUT THE AUTHOR 64

BIBLIOGRAPHY AND RESOURCES 67

Introduction
WHO MOVED MY PULPIT?
WHO MOVED MY PEW?

I am reminded of a book written years ago entitled Who Moved My Cheese by Spencer Johnson. This funny story was framed in a maze, and featured four characters; two mice, Sniff and Scurry, and two humans, Hem and Haw. The characters were faced with the varied dilemmas that are an inevitable part of life and at some point, realize the need to adjust their attitude and behavior so they could see their situation begin to improve. In short, the story of these four characters offer some invaluable lessons on dealing with CHANGE!

On their journey through the maze, they were met with some wonderful opportunities, including the discovery of a large stockpile of cheese. As you might imagine, this excited Sniff and Scurry. At other times, opportunities presented themselves as options to change direction. Sniff and Scurry were able to quickly adjust and continue their journey. However, Hem and Haw reacted very differently to change as opposed to Scuff and Scurry! Those less tangible opportunities; "signs along the way" or "handwriting on the wall," were often overlooked by Hem and Haw.

In a summary of the book, the author Spencer Johnson (Johnson and Library, 2007) states,

> "But the two have very different attitudes toward their situation. The humans Hem and Haw take the cheese for granted, assuming it will always be there. By contrast, the mice stay alert to their surroundings. They notice that the quality and supply of the cheese are slowly dwindling."

There are two important morals of this story that are relevant to the book you are reading today. They are:

1. In a state of complacency or fear, there is a tendency to resist, complain, and deny the need to **change.**

2. Adjusting attitude and behavior can cause situations to **change.**

Clearly, we have all experienced times when we did not pay attention to "signs along the way," then at the end of the journey when things turned out quite differently than expected, we ended up with our hands in the air asking, "What happened?" or "Who Moved My Cheese?" We realize what we thought would be forever and what we had begun to take for granted, was no longer there, or at least, not the same. Nevertheless, there is a remedy. As Sniff and Scurry did, and eventually Hem and Haw - we can adjust and continue to move forward.

Early one morning I was working in my office while listening to my morning inspirational music. Suddenly, the title of this book dropped in my spirit. I had not been thinking about authoring a book, and certainly not this one. Yet as a pastor, I have been looking for opportunities and strategies to shift our ministry to incorporate a variety of online experiences for our current members and for those that are newly joining our community in the wake of the COVID-19 Pandemic. As Ministry leaders, I am sure many of you are as well. Additionally, we all realize that so many congregants are struggling with our physical church doors being closed and the opening of what I like to call "house church," or in other words a "resurgence" – I believe, of small group ministry not unlike that found in the book of Acts, or perhaps modeled in more contemporary fashions as begun in the early 1960's.

It is my hope, that this guide will assist the many women and men of God in making the necessary adjustments so that we continue to lead the remarkable people that we have been given the privilege to lead. Many things have changed, but the Global Mission of the church has not. We must see that the Gospel of Jesus Christ is preached and taught around the world. We must fulfill the "work of the ministry" and do our part in revealing the existence and intention of a Holy God to His beloved creation.

Part One
WHO MOVED MY PULPIT?

This is really meant to be a quick read, so I will dive right in. Below, I'll share five things that have helped me as a pastor and have helped our ministry to transition as needed, during what I certainly consider to be some of the most challenging times I've experienced in my 58 years of life.

BE RELEVANT

I learned from a mentor in ministry the importance of being relevant in my pastoring and teaching. Merriam-Webster defines the word relevant as, "having significant and demonstrable bearing on the matter at hand." The Free Dictionary by Farlex puts it this way – "Meaningful or purposeful in current society or culture." Someone once said, if you are not relevant – you soon become obsolete!

For example, our ministry began to live stream our Sunday worship services over the Internet by way of Facebook and YouTube in early 2019. This decision was not made based upon the number of members/visitors to our brick and mortar location but was based upon the opportunity to share the Gospel with an expanded population – at very little cost. So, in the wake of recent changes to normal rules and regulations surrounding public gatherings, we were already in position to stay connected while quarantined and had fully embraced the use of technology for purposes of ministry.

Utilizing technology as a tool to reach people with the Gospel of Jesus Christ, in this day and age, is an example of Relevant ministry. Without saying, the content or substance must be solid, but to be clear, my point here is around method or strategy for delivery. We know the Gospel, but how do we spread the Gospel?

I recall in one of my seminary classes on ministry strategy, outreach, and communities – we were simply taught, "Find out where God is...and go there. Move there." The danger in not moving, is becoming obsolete.

When I think of my grandmother, I most often do so by recalling times that I sat in her living room/kitchen, which was one large room. She has gone on to be with the Lord for many years now, and her home no longer exists as it was, but even now as I sit writing at my kitchen table, I see her room with a hodgepodge of items; dishes, furniture, gadgets, and of course, a few faded pictures on her walls. I remember well how many of those items were quite dusty – she lived in the rural area of Mississippi and the roads to her home were gravel. Yet, they were proudly on display as if she had gotten them only yesterday. I am sure they met some need, but it was clear they were no longer in any shape to be effective in fulfilling the need they had been designed to fulfill. They were no longer usable – they were obsolete. Newer models and highly effective gadgets were available...

Yet, she had chosen to hang on to these!

In the church, it has been easy for us to fall into routines and comfort. If there has been nothing to cause us to change, shift or try something different, we generally don't. In fact, I believe we have seen the exodus of many of our millennial generation, simply because we did not take the time to incorporate different worship methods, music, and not to mention technology which I will talk about in the next chapter.

I am reminded of a discussion that I had within a ministry where I served as assistant pastor for a few years. I shared the need to help our congregants see that volunteers were needed not only as Sunday School teachers or Choir/Music ministry persons, but in the areas of finances, health, and technology as well. I believe whole-heartedly that these talents, skills, and capabilities empowered by Holy Spirit is what enables the church to remain relevant and accomplish its missing in an ever-changing world. Accordingly, I believe these talents and skills are not honored and supported enough by church leadership, and we have not done well in seeing and helping our congregants see these different, less obvious gifts, as valuable. Thus, our approach to health and mental wellness, our approach to the internet and online ministry, as well as our approach and management of finances is often outdated and, in many situations, lacking all together. Then, in comes COVID-19! Hopefully, our 2020 Vision we spoke so highly of in 2019 will now allow us to see the value I am referring to!

In Isaiah 43:19, the word of the Lord says,

> *"See, I am doing a new thing! Now it springs up; do you not perceive it? I am making a way in the wilderness and streams in the wasteland."*

Let me encourage you to go back and reflect on the handwriting on the wall that perhaps has been there for years. Be honest with yourself about some things you saw coming but procrastinated on or simply chose not to address. It is time to make some **changes**. Ask Holy Spirit for the strategies for your Ministry as well as considering those He led me to share in this guide. Look closely, see what plans you can implement right away, and how you can assemble teams to design and implement others soon.

Look to the many non-traditional, or perhaps what are typically considered 'non-spiritual' gifts within your congregation, and see where you can activate them to be a blessing to the ministry as a whole, and to help move you from obsolescence to a relevant, effective ministry force that's able to ride out the waves of the days ahead.

EMBRACE TECHNOLOGY

There is so much I could say about technology but let me level-set first. My formal background and bachelor's degree are in Information Technology and I have worked with computers and computer users for the last 30 years. My specialty is End-user Support and Training. With that said, some of my funniest work-related memories have been with customers who knew just enough about technology to be dangerous. Most times they accepted little proactive guidance but were quick to call you when something did not "work," and very hesitant to give you the full story leading up to their present predicament!

Today, all people are using Technology in one way or the other. When it comes to ministry, your church may not be online, but you can bet your current members are, and your potential members *certainly* are. Gone are the days where we sit and wait for people to enter our physical doors. Now, we are equipped with the means and technological advancements necessary to reach people *outside the four walls* – whether it be through a text, a phone call, an email newsletter, a podcast, a YouTube video, an Instagram story... the options are endless. With recent legislation regarding access to high-speed internet in rural or less densely populated areas, more people, have access to the Internet via a smartphone or computer.

Like most other things, technology has a multitude of uses, and not all are godly. However, lets decide to make the difference, to flood the airways with the Gospel of Jesus Christ. This... is going where the people are – This... is a powerful method of advancing the Kingdom of God and fulfilling the mission of the church!

In their blog article "14 Church Statistics You Need To Know For 2020",https://reachrightstudios.com/church-statistics-2020/ Reach Right statistics show that: 57% of the world uses the Internet and 45% of the population uses social media. There are 3.4 billion people using social media regularly.

Nowadays, technology is absolutely one of the ways we can see the message of the gospel go into "Jerusalem, and in all Judaea, and Samaria, and to the utmost of the earth" (Acts 1:8). Technology can enlarge our tent stakes right from our living room, and in the case of the Covid-19 pandemic, technology is the tool that has given us the ability to continue to reach our congregants and to fulfill our mission in this earth realm to our communities. You must invest your time and your treasure in being up to date with technology thus maintaining that connection between people and aiding the flow of ministry into the home as homes, backyards, and front porches are being transformed into sanctuaries. Glory to God!!!!

Below, I briefly discuss a few of the tools that I am using to remain 'technology relevant' in this time, and I am also providing some helpful links as well.

In preparation to host virtual meetings and/or livestream; you will need:

1. A webcam
2. Meeting software and/or
3. an account on your streaming platform(s) of choice
4. External microphone (optional, but recommended)
5. Lighting – (should be positioned on both sides of the subject, never just behind or in front.)
6. A Computer, Tablet, or Cell Phone

*Note – these options/directions provide you with the basics in terms of software and equipment and will suffice if you are streaming from your home, office, or small meeting space. If you desire to have a full-scale setup within your church sanctuary, more extensive lighting and or additional cameras may be necessary. You will be presently surprised though, with what you can do with very little equipment and minimal financial investment.

ZOOM is one of several tools you can use to host online meetings and webinars. It also works well for recording or livestreaming Sunday or Mid-Week settings. One of our pastors recently hosted an online Youth Conference with **ZOOM**, and in October 2020, **ZOOM** is our platform of choice at the ARC for our yearly leadership conference – LEADERCAMP 2020. (Register today at https://leadercamp2020.eventbrite.com).

This software is relatively inexpensive, and there are several levels of account memberships from free account to those with minimal monthly payments starting at about $15 a month. This tool can be used on a Windows or MacOS computer, tablet/IPAD, or on a cell phone. That is really one of the notable things about the tool – it works smoothly across all platforms/devices.

I began using **ZOOM** about 6 years ago when several people had problems connecting to telephone conference lines or were experiencing extra fees for connecting to ministry conference calls I was hosting. **ZOOM** makes it easy and free for uses to connect via their telephone or other device. When setting up an online meeting all it takes is simply a click of a button to add access for telephone dial in, and/or access via the Internet. If you're interested in learning more about **ZOOM**, here is a link to a <u>free ZOOM Video Teaching</u> (https://www.youtube.com/watch?v=5kxhvjiFCp8&feature=youtu.be) I recorded in March of 2020.

Streamyard. Streamyard is one of several tools on the market used specifically to record or livestream a broadcast. By the way, the term livestream means "to stream digital data (such as audio or video material) that is delivered continuously and is usually intended for immediate processing or playback."

One of the benefits of this tool is you can broadcast to more than one platform simultaneously. For example, if you want your livestream to go out over YouTube *and* Facebook simultaneously, (Multistreaming) you can set up both accounts in **Streamyard**. Pricing for **Streamyard** is very reasonable and begins with a free account and extends to multiple levels which are reasonably priced based upon how many platforms you want to stream to simultaneously and other options like High Definition 1080P streaming.

I also really like **Streamyard's** *Banners and Overlays* features. Banners can be easily used to add text onscreen with your livestream. For example, while I am preaching from the book of Proverbs, I add my scriptures or preaching points easily, each one on its own "banner". You may also have someone else logged in to the broadcast with you, and they can control these onscreen features. Overlays allow you to display flyers on screen and create other frames around your image in the broadcast. Lastly, **Streamyard** has features that allow you to see comments that people are making in real time, and you can respond right from within the interface. Even though this is not something I use on Sunday mornings, it is helpful during informal, quick livestreams."

In addition to live streaming, **Streamyard** can be used to simply record your broadcast. At times, I record my Sunday broadcast on Saturday, save it, and then upload it to **YouTube** or other platforms. I then set the video to Premiere as if it was live (I will discuss this in the **YouTube** section).

The process itself is pretty simple, and there are several help files and video tutorials. You simply log in, name your broadcast, choose the platforms you will stream to, and set the date and time. You can also set up the broadcast in advance of your livestream. This then creates a pretty nice-looking image that you can share across social media and **YouTube** to advertise your livestream and when it will start. If you're interested in learning more, here's a quick link to Streamyard https://streamyard.com/resources/docs/getting-started/. Create your free account and check it out today!

YouTube Live. Most all of us are familiar with **YouTube**, and they have really enhanced their livestreaming features. You must use a desktop or laptop computer to stream live over **YouTube** if you have less than 1000 people subscribed to your **YouTub**e channel, and its features for doing so are easy to set up. Like most people I'd begun to do some **Facebook Live** videos, but was really lead to focus on **YouTube** because people tend to go to **YouTube** for more concise information (as well as entertainment) and its searching features and overall setup/interface make it easy for people to go back at a later date and time and find the information that you presented. There are many how-to videos out there on livestreaming on **YouTube** so I have not produced one, but here is a great link from Google - https://support.google.com/youtube/answer/2474026?hl=en with instructions. You might also check out this article - https://www.thegospelcoalition.org/article/livestream-church-service-practical-guide/ by Phil Thompson published in the Gospel Coalition, which gives some ideas specifically about **livestreaming church services**. When it comes to **YouTube**, statistics show that:

- YouTube has over two billion users
- Millennials are the biggest audience
- Over a billion hours of video are watched daily
- Over 70% of views come from mobile devices (another key trait of millennial viewers)

Think about this! How could we NOT make us of this FREE platform to reach others for the sake of the Gospel!

Websites. This next area of the pulpit I want to share is the website. Your website should become the primary place to access everything that you are doing in ministry. If you want to connect your

Facebook page, livestreams, small groups, etc., create a **central hub** so that it is easy for you and viewers to access or find what they are looking for, all in one place.

During this season we have invested financially into building our website to be inclusive and support all the platforms I have described above, as well as an embedded learning management system and registration system that can assist with various workshops and events. There are many companies out there that offer these services. I do not have any particular recommendations for you; however, I *will* say that making it easier for people to find you and everything that you're doing is key. You can find us at http://www.thearcinternational.org/, for an example, and I hope you will create a FREE account and become a part of our online community for ministry.

RETEACH AND RELEASE

It has been the re-teaching of our church body and releasing them to minister within their homes and communities that has helped our ministry to not only sustain, but to grow during the pandemic and quarantine of 2020.

Perhaps you've already noticed part 2 of this book, *Who Moved My Pew?* Well, just as the pastor is asking "Who Moved My Pulpit?", our congregants now wonder "*Who Moved My Pew?* Or in other words, *how will I have church now that I cannot get to my pew?* You know, my favorite seat in the church, the one that my family brought and has my family name etched on a Gold Plaque attached to the side of it. I'm not saying this to demean that practice at all, but what I am saying is **We** as pastors are responsible for ensuring that our congregants understand how they should *continue* to worship God, in spite of the absence or delay of more typical or traditional practices, and that **They** are the **Church**. We should all study the word of God together -teaching one another, praying together, having communion together, and allowing the varied gifts of Holy Spirit, the laying of hands, prophecy, and all of the others to flow as the Holy Spirit leads. I have made it a focus in this time to provide several teachings on the importance of our relationship with Holy Spirit, Discernment, and other practices I mentioned above that are a part of corporate worship. I believe it is also important to discuss and be open to what this all looks like as more and more people take the opportunity to minister in more one on one and small group settings.

The transition to using technology to listen to the word of God has been challenging for many. Think about it. Most all of us are used to sitting in a physical classroom setting, with a human being before us as we learn. To specifically address this challenge, we have also begun teaching sessions within our Bible study which simply talk about how to learn and "receive" using technology and recorded messages. We have made ourselves available to assist all that need assistance in installing or configuring their computers or downloading apps to their phones. This is God's work too – making the gospel more easily accessible to a wide variety of people and tailoring to people's specific needs. It shows the care, consideration, and heart of God.

I recorded a video in August 2020 entitled House Church! [Here's a link - https://youtu.be/ts1Wwf4Jb_o](https://youtu.be/ts1Wwf4Jb_o) if you'd like to check it out. Note that this content is also covered in Part 2 of this book, *"Who Moved My Pew?"*

Here are a few key things to remember related to re-teaching and re-leasing!

1. Engage those in your congregation with those amazing skills and non-traditional gifts to teach your congregants to use technology for purposes of Bible Study and online learning in general. Expose them to tools and apps like **YouTube**. Trust me, you will likely find many are already using **YouTube** and Google,

but for other reasons. Personally, I have enjoyed using YouTube as a source for learning DIY home projects and gardening.

2. Teach and Learn to "consider the source" Guide your congregants in making wise choices of who they are receiving information from. Frankly, it would not be wise of us to think that our congregants are *only* listening to our broadcast on Sundays and Wednesdays for Bible study. A study from Barna Group revealed,

"While a majority of churchgoers tend to stick with a single congregation (63% churched adults, 72% practicing Christians), a sizable minority is at least occasionally attending other churches, including nearly two in five churched adults (38%) and one-quarter of practicing Christians (27%)." This study was done between December 5-18, 2019, using a nationally representative panel. The rate of error for this data is +/- 2.2% at the 95% confidence level.

With that said, you know as I do that not all information made readily available or presented is necessarily accurate or true. One thing about the Internet we must always be careful of, is that it is "open source". In other words, anyone can create a webpage or blog and present their thoughts or teachings. Anyone can record a video with a Bible in their hand and call it the Word of God. However, not every voice is a voice influenced by Holy Spirit. So how do congregants discern fact from fiction? Truth from deceit? You must give guidance around that. You must spend some time re-teaching the importance of an active relationship with Holy Spirit. There are noteworthy and reliable Bible Study sites/apps you should share with your congregants. You must remind congregants that along with a charismatic delivery of the preached word, a lifestyle of character and integrity is paramount. What do we know about the "teachers" we watch or listen to over the Internet? We must have clear teaching and discussion around Prophecy. A prophetic utterance has a way of drawing people like I have not seen before. The issue is, is it truly the voice of God? How do you know?

You must be sure to emphasize constant meditation on God's word and recognizing divine connections in the life of the believer. You must empower your congregants to move through this time of shifting and shaking so that they may have the godly wisdom, knowledge, and tools to make wise choices and decisions regarding the leadership voices in their life. There will be more than one, I assure you! And the goal should simply be to make sure that those voices are spreading God's truth, and His truth alone.

3. Releasing. There are far too many believers that feel that they can no longer take communion because they are not at the church with their pastor or ministers serving them communion. Please release them from that belief, and from any beliefs around the need to have that nice little foil cup with the wafer and the juice all in a packet. Remind them that these are simply symbols that represent His Body and His Blood, and that they can have Communion as "oft" as they desire to – with a glass of water and a saltine cracker, and that Communion can be "self-service."

Encourage them to study and pray together in their homes. Suggest books or lessons they can use for the children and adults. Please let them know they have the freedom to minister to one another at their houses, in their small groups they may be quarantining with, or with a neighbor who may be in dire need of someone to pray with them for healing or financial provision.

Please help people to understand that if they are in their communities praying for others, it is not necessary to lay a physical hand upon them. Holy Spirit moves outside of the realm of the physical. As we pray for one another over the phone from miles and miles away, the spirit of the Lord moves and manifests, because of the heart and the belief of the individual(s) praying and His will in the situation.

In short, we can teach our congregants how to gather at whatever time works for their family and to sit and listen to the word of God together. They should have discussion around it, pray, sing, and have fellowship over a meal. At the ARC, we are forming small groups, and teaching our congregants how to gather using tools like **ZOOM**. You may choose to have a straightforward way for families or other small groups that form to check in with your ministry administrators, to report on the health and well-being of the members of families. You might create a simple email address dedicated to this very purpose, or even a quick form on your website. These are just a few ideas.

Help your church family learn to worship in small groups in their homes. It is important to be able to adjust and adapt successfully in these uncertain times, and we must model and encourage them in the process. Heck, you might even want to give them a copy of this book!

AUTOMATE FINANCIAL PROCESSES

This by far is one of the most difficult conversations that many are having at this time. I don't know that there is any one perfect solution that will fit every single church. Instead, my goal is to give you some strategy and talk a little bit about tools that continue to help congregants give financially, and then to encourage you moving forward because many of you will have some extremely difficult decisions to make.

You may be familiar with, but have not yet embraced, 'electronic' giving. Some have been hesitant due to fears around security and privacy. This is absolutely a valid concern. However, there are ways to give that are safe and secure, which have been tried and tested for several years. I will share a few options, but as a disclaimer, I am not here to promote any one platform.

From your website

If you have a website, it is very simple to team up with **PayPal® - Official Site** and put a button or link on your website that people can click on. From there they can make their payment to your ministry via credit/debit card or check. There are **PayPal** personal accounts and business accounts. Be sure to set up a business account for your ministry. There are also fees involved, just as there are for any business that is transacting with credit cards; however, they are charged only when a transaction occurs, and there are options within **PayPal** to determine whether or not the fees are passed on to the person giving or if the organization will absorb the fee. Your choice.

PayPal has been around since 1998 and is fairly simple to use. What I have described above can literally be configured in no more than 30 minutes. If you do not want to configure it yourself, it is worth it to pay someone a nominal fee to make this small change on your website which will allow your congregants to give. Who knows, there is likely a business owner in your ministry that already uses **PayPal** and can quickly set this up for you! Or, call upon some of those "non-traditional" gifted millennials to give you a hand!

Let me also mention that with a **PayPal** account you can even establish an email address and a link that can be sent to someone in a text message, and they can click that link and make a payment to you through **PayPal**. It is not necessary that they have an account set up, but I do believe in this day and time it is more secure for everyone to take advantage of creating a free account on their platform and then proceeding to use the app.

Lastly, **PayPal** has a plethora of reports that you can use to generate 'End of Year' giving information for your congregants, as well as tools to track your spending and purchases via **PayPal**. I have used this tool for ministry, business, and personal use for at least the last ten years. I have not experienced any issue that was not swiftly resolved, and in fact, I can count the issues experienced on one hand.

Mobile Apps

SQUARE. If you are an entrepreneur, you are likely familiar with **SQUARE** in that many use this technology to accept credit cards on the go. **SQUARE** is also the owner of the popular money app, **Cash App**, actually named **Square Cash**, which is used for sending and receiving payments. However, there is no ability to produce reports, etc. that you would need as a ministry collecting donations. You are issued an account with a unique username, called a *cashtag*, which customers can use to send payments to you or your business. Along with the *cashtag*, **SQUARE** gives **Cash App** business users a payment page with a custom URL. Customers can pay by clicking a link on your website or visiting cash.me/YourCashtag. Just like hashtags or social media handles, *cashtags* are suitable for adding to your business card and marketing campaigns to let customers know v Cash is an option for payment." See the resources section at the end of this book for a helpful website on using CASHAPP for business.

If they already have an account, customers can send payments right from the app, which is available for iOS and Android, but an account is not required to pay through your cash.me page. All transactions incur a 2.75 percent fee, but deposits are free if you do not need access to the money right away. If you want your money deposited immediately, you can use the Instant Transfer feature; Square charges 1.5 percent of the balance for this method.

While I have only recently begun to use Cash App, I only use it sparingly for personal transactions. For business I much prefer **SQUARE**. It operates much like **PayPal** in features and reporting and has proven to be safe and reliable. It is definitely worth investigating to see if it will work for your ministry. By the way, **PayPal** and **SQUARE** can both be used to accept credit card payments over the telephone.

Giving Apps

Reporting and tracking donations are critical for a ministry, and automation of these processes can save the pastor and administrative staff precious time and money and aid in accuracy. Thus, I would suggest you choose a tool or app that provides reporting and tracking features that you need. In December 2019, we chose to introduce a Giving App to our congregation that is specifically designed for churches! Previously, we utilized PayPal. We solely made this decision upon the church/ministry/nonprofit related features of this giving app. I want to be certain to say that we have experienced no problems with PayPal – and continue to use it for many of our events. You should do your research; and find the software/app that is right for your organization from a technical and a financial standpoint. Here is a great website article from Outreach.com - https://outreach.com/blog/best-church-online-giving-platforms/ which will give you some information on a few choices.

At the ARC, we selected Tithe.ly - https://get.tithe.ly/ Giving App for our ministry. Giving apps tend to have great reporting features, and many include other features you can upgrade to like "text to give" or "messaging." These features allow the user to simply send a text message to give, they send e-mail receipts, and can even handle refunds. Messaging features allows the ministry to quickly send mass e-mail or text messages that can service as reminders for service times or events. Often there are nominal monthly fees for the organization to set up these features (it may be around $20-$30 per month) but it is well worth it if it easily allows your congregation and visitors to give and communicate remotely.

The other point to be made in this is that when you are going to embed a new process, especially involving technology, into your ministry, and it is something that's going to be used by everyone, you need to take the time to teach people how to use it. For example, we dedicated four weeks in the month of December 2019 to provide written instructions and videos (all of which were provided by the vendor), to our congregants. We gave assistance in downloading the app and configuring the settings on their phones if needed. There is no charge for the app itself, and this is true for most all giving apps. These critical four weeks gave us time to make sure things were working correctly and that people were comfortable in using the technology.

Everyone loved the immediate receipts that were sent, and not do the individuals receive a receipt, but the organization itself immediately is notified via e-mail when a donation is given. I do realize that some of us have older congregants that may be less inclined to use an app on their phone, but many of our *Seasoned Saints* do text, and might be open to use this new method. Most of these apps also allow you to set up "recurring giving", meaning the individual can complete the initial setup, choose an amount to give as well as the frequency, and then only has to touch the application again if they want to make a change to the normal amount that they are giving or desire to cancel their giving. This will make it easy for those who do not want to constantly fuss about technicalities every time. It can be a 'one and done' process.

Another plus with our **giving app** is you can embed a link on your website or set it up on a IPAD so that it works like an ATM Kiosk. So, however a person chooses to give, via text, from your website, in person on a KIOSK, it is all going into the same record-keeping application – and we can feel confident that the transactions are documented and secure.

That said, there may still be those that will not want to utilize technology at all. You may still have to simply provide a P.O. Box where a check can be mailed, and you may even decide that you're going to prepare self-addressed, stamped envelopes and mail them out to those in your congregation to be of assistance to them.

Financial Transparency

More than ever, it is important in this season to continue to have transparent financial meetings with your church body. Certainly, I hope this has already been your practice. We currently have these meetings on a quarterly basis. It is important to let your congregants know that financial responsibilities like mortgage/rent and utilities continue to occur, even though you may not be meeting in that physical building at this time. Share additional financial responsibilities the ministry has had to take on to deal with technology purchases that are allowing you to continue to minister to them (coming into the home by way of technology). I believe wholeheartedly in taking care of business in ministry, and with these practices already in place there should not really a need to transition to them during this time of crisis. But nonetheless, these are still important reminders just in case. I hope you are hearing what I am saying. These are really issues of integrity that every ministry needs to attend to at all times.

In the concluding chapter I will talk a little about **Outreach**. You have likely invested funds or donations to outreach and a variety of other areas during this period of the COVID-19 pandemic, but be transparent about your investment and if there is a need for more to be designated in that area, give to it.

Whether it be normal expenses, outreach, or greater decisions (like for us – how long we will continue to pay monthly rent on a space we are unable to use at this time) it can and *should* be shared with your members. While you and your leadership team are responsible for making the final decisions, do not underestimate important input and creative ideas that might come from others. Plus, having these conversations with the larger body is a great way of continuing to stay connected. Everyone wants to feel they are being heard and that their opinion is valued.

RENEW YOUR FOCUS ON OUTREACH

As I prepare to close Part One of this book, I thought it very important to talk about **Outreach**. I am sure you've heard the rumor over the last few months – that the church has finally come "outside of the four walls." Based upon the demographics of your ministry, its size, and its vision, **outreach** during this time will look different from ministry to ministry. However, the bottom line is that your **outreach** should be active and growing during this time.

It is key to have a way for your congregants to submit information about any benevolent or **outreach** needs, and it is important to have a plan around how your ministry can reach out and touch the community. Here are some ideas that we have put into place as well as ideas that I have seen that I thought were simply amazing. Oh, one last thing – collaboration is the key to success; after all, what better time than the present for the Body of Christ to work together as one?

Sharing Information and Resources

More times than none, resources for help are available, but getting the word out is the issue. I have encountered ministries positioned and ready to do amazing work in the community, but no one knows about them or the program opportunity. Thus, in this season we have worked more diligently to share information across our social media platforms, text message groups, and of course by word of mouth. Information about resources, such as food giveaways, health-related notices as we prepare to go back to school, and programs to help parents with home instruction and/or opportunities for work-from-home employment are all crucial to relay to our communities.

As a pastor, I began to host a monthly Pastors Unity call with the sole purpose of unifying those that would participate so that we might share ideas, strategies, and collaborate on outreach. During the initial calls, we taught a **ZOOM** class and had a medical professional on the line to provide some guidance surrounding COVID-19 and proper safety precautions. This was much needed, especially around April 2020, when many churches were considering opening their doors to the masses for Resurrection Sunday. We have taken the time to dedicate a page on our website specifically for pastors and church leaders, where we continue to upload helpful resources, videos, and presentations which can guide them through some of the challenges that we are all experiencing at this time. You can click here - http://www.thearcinternational.org/pastors-unity-fellowship.html to access that page, or see the link in our Resources section at the end of this book.

You do not have to reinvent the wheel, and you may not be the provider of the resource. Helping to get the word out and sharing as much information as you can in the simplest way possible is greatly needed and can make a world of a difference for someone in need.

Collaboration

When it comes to outreach, we don't have to go at it alone. Collaboration is a proven method to move forward at a faster pace, and in this instance, our mission is Kingdom – and with a purpose to minister and aid people in a variety of ways. Of course, different ministries have different resources, and congregants, who all have unique skills, talents, and abilities that can contribute to the cause in different ways. When the Body of Christ collaborates, or Unifies...we are able to do amazing work in the community.

If you have the heart and hands to participate in food give-away ministry but do not have the location or space, why not team up with someone that does? Why not team up with a local food bank or pantry? Perhaps your contribution at this time is not in the distribution of the food, but perhaps you can help a local pantry pack boxes or trucks that hold the goods or resources. Perhaps you are assisting with communication and connecting people with resources for food, sharing the information. There are a multitude of ideas such as this I could expand upon.

The other benefit of collaboration is that it reinforces greater connection between churches and ministries in the community. During the last six months, Holy Spirit has continually whispered this phrase to me – "Together is the way through." It always has been. There has long been a great a need for more unity in the Body of

Christ, and greater collaboration between churches and non-profit ministries that serve local communities. What better time than now?

Romans 12:4-5

> "4 For just as each of us has one body with many members, and these members do not all have the same function,
>
> 5 so in Christ we, though many, form one body, and each member belongs to all the others."

Connecting

I suspect we might all be surprised at the number of people that have been quarantining alone. VOX Media reported,

> "The most precious commodity these days is human contact." (coronavirus-covid-19-social distancing closed circle, single-alone)

For sure, the church will need to be prepared to address instances of extreme isolation and depression amongst our congregants and in our communities, not to mention trauma. BARNA posted a great article regarding this entitled: "Do Pastors Feel Well-Equipped to Help Congregants Heal from Trauma - http://www.barna.com/research/pastors-trauma-care?".

Could it be that a component of our outreach at this time might simply be *Connecting?* Assembling volunteers from your ministry to take part in a phone tree, whose focus is on reaching out to people quarantining alone can help reassure and encourage those who feel lonely, forgotten about, or are in a depressive/anxious state. This also becomes a way to engage your congregants in meaningful volunteer work at this time. Many may think that having assignments to call and check on people might be insignificant, but that is so far from the truth. This is of immense importance and can make a difference in one's mental, emotional, physical, and not to mention spiritual health.

I am reminded of a friend who was diagnosed with COVID-19. He lived alone. He was on a Face-Time call with a friend, and that person noticed he did not look well and highly encouraged him to go to the doctor immediately. On our own, we have a way of talking ourselves out of things that we need to do, and in isolation, it is easy for fear and depression to set in. "Connecting ministry," is crucial!

Another way we have practiced connecting is through drive-by and outdoor visits. These are times when we may drive by another's home and simply sit outside on a porch or in the yard. These are short visits, maybe 15 to 20 minutes, and not designed to invade anyone's living space, but just to *connect*. It is during these times that for some we can do a quick drop-off of supplies or groceries, or maybe even have communion.

This is certainly not meant to be an exhaustive list of ideas and practices for pastors and church leaders, but it is an excellent beginning if you have found yourself stuck and struggling to move forward and be effective in ministry in this season. I can guarantee you that as you begin to move forward in doing even one or two of these small things, the Father will illuminate your next steps in a way you would have never experienced, had you not begun by taking the first step.

Just as I shared how instrumental the church can be in sharing resources to help the community, you must know that there are those the Father has assigned to assist and equip *you* – Pastors and Church Leaders – to move through this uncomfortable season. There is grace for His Church. God is Sovereign, and He is right here to walk us through the new things He is doing. There is a way in the wilderness and a stream in the wasteland. Isaiah 43:19 says: "**See, I am doing a new thing! Now it springs up; do you not perceive it? I am making a way in the wilderness and streams in the wasteland.**"

Part Two
WHO MOVED MY PEW?

House Church! How You do that?

I want to talk to the saints, about what I call "House Church." In other words, how do I have church, in my home? This has been on my heart for a few months and I see the struggles. I see us missing those corporate "moves of God." I see us trying hard to re-create that atmosphere at home, and then frankly, I see many more who have not tried anything at all. Those that are really struggling with this whole thing, you have been going to church every Sunday for 5, 10, 50 years, and now, nothing. I hope you will read further, because I believe what the Lord has given me to share will help you, make you laugh, change your perspective on some things, and frankly, free you to be The Church!

I do not know of any other way to start this conversation, other than to begin with a reminder that the church is not a building, but a physical temple yielded to God, allowing Him to fully reside in and guide our lives. So, if this is you, and you are alive (you must be; you are reading this book) then God's church is alive and well. To God be the Glory!

I believe that *you* have what you need on the inside of you to move forward in this time, and create an atmosphere of worship, teaching, prayer, whatever is needed – right there in your own home. The goal here is not necessarily to duplicate or recreate what we did in our corporate gatherings, but it *is* to create an empowering, uplifting, healing, spiritual atmosphere with and for our families. It is an opportunity to have some real discussion and do some real witnessing, right there in our homes, or on the porch with a neighbor.

I get it, we miss our *Pew!* Our seat we sit in each Sunday – the one that has that etched plaque and was donated by family, the one no one else better sit in! What else? We miss being with our church friends, our shouting and dancing partners! We miss being in the midst of praise and worship and getting hyped up with the music. We miss our choir, even though we thought they sang the same song too many times last month, but we miss that. So, I wanted to talk about those things.

The purpose of this book is not to prophesy or make any promises about the future, dates, times, or methods the church will take on in years to come, but it is to share the direction I sense the Lord has given for now especially as it relates to the forming of small groups for the purpose of ministry, and in a real and practical way how my family and I, as well as the members of my church, are embracing and being obedient to this direction, and what it can look like for you. The fact that WE are the Church must spring forth in this season like never before, and the reality that the walls have come down to literally propel the church into the community is one that must be embraced, or at the least, considered. It is time for us to make some adjustments and time for us to truly make changes in some areas.

As it relates to small group ministry, one thing I find quite interesting is that this really is not new! The book of Acts, Chapter 2, talks about church at that time and while there were temples, there were many churches and small groups that met in homes. As I studied this in the word of God and in other commentaries, I found something I believe can be a blessing to all of us at this time.

First, there are elements to our church experience that I want to identify. They are:

- Worship
- practice of the spiritual gifts
- teaching
- prayer
- fellowship
- evangelism
- The Lord's Supper
- and Baptism.

We are the church, right? So that is exactly why we need to have this conversation! All those things I listed above do not need a big, fancy building. They don't require large groups of individuals, and they don't require ordained ministers or pastors to be in the midst...(I'm getting in trouble here and I know it, but I promise it's "Good Trouble" (Sen. John Lewis)). We do not need a well-decorated space, an elaborate music setup or videographer complete with colorful lights, and a platform, and we do not need to be dressed in our Sunday best. No? then what *does* it take?

It takes Believers! It takes those who have an intimate relationship with God the Father and are led and directed by Holy Spirit. It takes those who are passionate about Worshipping Him and attending to His purposes in this earth realm. It takes those that will walk this earth in His image and likeness come what may, understanding that the purpose of the church has always been to be out and to move in the midst of the people (as did Jesus Christ) and not the other way around. Think about it like this - what if it was another year or so before it is safe for all to gather in large groups? What about those that have for years been house bound because of other challenges - physical, financial, etc. People have been dealing with these issues and learning how to navigate them long before the COVID-19 pandemic. Did the Father intend for His purposes to come to a halt then (under more 'normal' circumstances)? It is no different now. Is the Kingdom of God to stop expanding? Is the Father not healing and delivering any longer? Is He no longer worthy to be praised?

This is not the case; this is not the truth. The truth is, God is more present and active than ever. I believe that in this season He really desires the believer to step out, to put into practice all they have been receiving, and all that word and teaching many have been feasting on for many years.

It is interesting; we trust medical doctors who have been trained for 10 years or so with our very life. We believe they must be ready because they graduated. What about you, is it not graduation time yet? How many years has it been that you have been continuing to receive…isn't it time for us to begin giving? How many years have you been strictly in a following mode? Well, now your family needs you, your community needs you, and the world needs you. It is time to step out, take action, and lead!

With that said, so you like to sing and you miss that choir? Well, find one of those tracks on **YouTube** that will allow you to sing along with it and sing your song. Or just simply sing along to someone's video or your favorite worship song. Get your kids together and sing along. Listen, make this fun, and do not make it so formal. Give you and your family a break on the church clothes! The important thing is for you to gather together and understand that when two or three are gathered in His name, He is right there in the midst. So whenever you are going to do it, whether it's tomorrow morning or whether it's later this evening, get your folks that are in the house with you and gather together, lift up the name of Jesus and watch what happens.

WORSHIP

In our home, 30 minutes before our Sunday broadcast we begin with praise and worship, and then prayer. As a pastor, some Sundays I broadcast live, but many times I record my Sunday broadcast on Saturday morning, and through the mystery of technology, I premier the video as LIVE on Sunday morning. This allows me to enjoy the Sunday setting with my family. Speaking of technology, isn't it great? We can have whoever we want to minister praise and worship that morning, whether it is Darrel Coley, Tasha Cobbs, or Hillsong! Might be BB & CC Winans or Donnie McClurkin – you choose! **YouTube** is your friend. Set the amount of time you will spend, the songs you and your family like, and play them as the family begins to gather in your living room, even in your kitchen. The important thing is to gather those in your home, whether it is two of you, eight of you, or just the one of you.

What we are doing here is bringing a little structure to this time that has since been lost or lacking. After a few weeks, they may begin to catch on, even look forward to it. As for my family, sometimes we fix a little coffee, eat a little bit of fruit, and dance before the Father! After that there is prayer and intersession before the Word of God is shared.

TEACHING

Teaching can happen in several ways. If your ministry currently has a weekly broadcast, your teaching time might begin by listening to the broadcast together and then follow that time with some discussion. Or, you might select someone in your home – even rotate this responsibility – to lead a brief lesson from their devotion that past week or from one of many devotional books you can purchase online, even access for free online. You do not have to reinvent the wheel. In that we are pastors, we do begin with our own broadcast. We are listening, we are taking notes, and since it's recorded, we pause and rewind if and when needed. We often incorporate other Bible teachers who we admire, starting with our own Apostle, Dr. Kluane Spake of SWORD Ministries.

One especially important element of our teaching time is discussion. We do this within our ministry when we meet in person as well, so we continue it now that we are in our home. We talk about what we just listened to, so that we understand how we will apply it to our lives. We ask questions of one another, and we go further searching in the Word of God for answers if that is what we need to do. We sit and talk, until we each feel we have peace. Then, we pray together, and we ask the Lord for His plan for us as individuals going into the next week.

PRAYER AND PRACTICE OF SPIRITUAL GIFTS

Prayer points are easy when you have had that discussion. It is a time when folks ask questions and identify areas where they might be struggling... a time when they ask for help. These become the beginning of the prayer points. There are times when a prophetic word will come forward. Praise the Lord. Thus, we just allow Him to move in that time the way He wants to move. As believers, we pray, lay hands on one another, and believe God will administer healing when needed – physical, mental, *and* emotional.

Now to all of you that might be saying, "Well, she's a pastor and her husband is a pastor." It is easy for them. Well, we are human beings, and just like you we are facing similar challenges and difficulties that come with the disruption to our normal routines and schedules. We have had our struggles, and have had to adjust, which is how I know it's possible. Yu should know that as congregants you have just as much responsibility to be dedicated and devoted to incorporating these techniques and worshipping God in these trying times as your pastors do. More importantly, know that you are Well Able!

So, let us keep moving forward. You do not have to be a pastor or minister to lay hands on someone else and decree healing over them. You need to be a Believer; God is on the inside of you. Holy Spirit will prophesy through you as He pleases – you do not have to be a Prophet, and because He *uses* you in that moment to prophesy, does not mean that you *are* a Prophet. It simply means that in this moment in time the Father desired a Rhema word to come forth and that He gave it to you to deliver. Let the Spirit of Prophecy flow!

1 Corinthians 14:31 says, "For you can all prophesy in turn so that everyone may be instructed and encouraged." Who does not need to be encouraged in this season? This is the foundational purpose of prophecy. It is to encourage, to edify to build up.

You can speak life over another person or their situation right there in your home. Do not allow anyone to suffer in their situation when you have the power of God active on the inside of you. SPEAK LIFE! Do not hold back; you do not have to have a ministerial license and have been to seminary school to lay hands on a person. You lay hands on them because you understand it is not you, but the power of God that works *through* you. God can and will use whomever He chooses, and He seeks those Believers who are will and make themselves available.

So, pray for that child. Pray for grandmamma, granddaddy, momma, daddy, whoever it is! You might even need to have your children lay hands on *you*. Pray over yourself as well! Is there someone sick in your home? Lay hands on them! Get some olive oil, vegetable oil, or Crisco! Put a little bit on the palm of your hand, lay hands on the intended individual, pray for them, and believe God to do the work.

COMMUNION: THE LORD'S SUPPER

Have Communion in your home. You do not need to have a pastor, an elder, or a licensed minister to serve you communion! Guess what, you do not even have to have those little cups, the one with the wafer on the top with the aluminum foil, that is hard to open. You do not have to have all that – you can have a glass of water, any kind of cracker or piece of bread, read scripture, and take communion. Look here – https://www.kingjamesbibleonline.org/Bible-Verses-About-Holy-Communion/ for a quick list of Scriptures regarding Jesus and Holy Communion.

You don't have to wait until 1st Sunday, but the word of the Lord says in 1 Corinthians 11:25,

> "In the same way, after supper he took the cup, saying, 'This cup is the new covenant in my blood; do this, whenever you drink it, in remembrance of me.'"

You can have communion anytime you want and as often as you want. Simply do it and let it be in remembrance of Him. Those things we use – the wine or the juice, the bread/cracker – those are simply symbols! They *represent* the body of Jesus Christ. They *represent* the blood of Jesus Christ. Use what you have, and do not deny yourself this personal experience of becoming one with Him, and one with the others who we share communion with. Do not deny your mother or father, or perhaps you have elders living with you - maybe you have your grandmother or grandfather living with you. Do not deny them communion time because you think, or they think it must be done in such a fashion. You have been prepared for this! You are ready for this! Sit down and have a talk with them. They may not receive what you are saying initially, but for those in your home that will – you all go forward and have communion. Allow God to work out the details with the others. I pray that pastors and leaders will support this effort, and I believe that you will see your entire family eventually begin to join in this special time.

In Bible study a few weeks ago, we talked about having church at home, and one of the young ladies shared that one Sunday she happened to go outside with a Bluetooth speaker and had church service playing. Guess what, her neighbors heard the sound of music and preaching. Before she knew it, her neighbors had come over from their house, and they were all in the yard (social distancing) yet having church! They all came out of their spiritual boxes, outside the 4 walls, and did something new and different!

We must come out of these strict manufactured routines, which really only serve to limit a greater move of God. We must come out of so many man-made rules, regulations, and guidelines that prevent us from experiencing the presence of God like never before. Be careful that you do not fall into the trap of believing God is dead, because you cannot gather in a church building. God is here, He is alive, and He is well. He is waiting to rise like never before on the inside of each and every one of you.

The gifts you have held bottled up on the inside of you because they would not call on you at your church; be free to exercise that gift now. Believe God and move forward as He directs right now, in your own home, with your own family. Step out and prophecy, decree healing, and lay hands on – right now in the name of Jesus. Watch God because it is not about you. It is not about your power, nor about your might. It never has been about you, but rather about Him and the fact that He's alive and well on the inside of you! You can see people and situations transformed in your home by just making the decision that you are going to gather where you are, with whomever is there. Decide you're going to step outside of the box that you have been in. This season God is leading us outside the box, and outside of the walls of the church. He is leading us outside of all our old routines and old habits that have not been a blessing to Him and have not benefited His people – the ones that have caused us to remain stagnant, inactive, and focused on trivial matters. He is trying to get us back to His Intention, the way he designed life for us originally. Do not miss it; don't miss the opportunity. With God you are ready, and you are able.

BAPTISM

Do you have a bathtub in your house? If there is someone in your home that desires to be saved and to be baptized, go to that bathroom, place them in that water or even over the edge of the tub, and speak the word of God over them and baptize them if that is their desire. You can do that! What? Yes, you can do that. Baptism is an outward symbol and confession of the inward reality of saving faith in Jesus Christ. It is a symbol of salvation, not the means of salvation.

Here are a few verses that show that baptism always follows saving faith. These are reprinted from Bible.org

> *Acts 2:41: "So then, those who had received his word were baptized ...."*
>
> *Acts 8:12: "But when they believed Philip preaching the good news about the kingdom of God and the name of Jesus Christ, they were being baptized, men and women alike."*
>
> *Acts 10:44, 46b-48a: "While Peter was still speaking these words, the Holy Spirit fell upon all those who were listening to the message.... Then Peter answered, 'Surely no one can refuse the water for these to be baptized who have received the Holy Spirit just as we*

did, can he?' And he ordered them to be baptized in the name of Jesus Christ."

EVANGELISM AND FELLOWSHIP

Somebody needs to be led to the Lord! After all, somebody led us! Somebody shared Christ with us and was instrumental in revealing God to us. Guess what? That is the work of the ministry that is referred to in Ephesians 4:11. As believers, it is our responsibility to ensure that Christ and Christ in us is revealed to others. So what about you? Are you ready? Do you feel able to lead someone else to Christ? Are you comfortable in sharing your testimony, and walking with someone to help them build their relationship with God? Can you share the Gospel of Jesus Christ and the importance of His death, burial, and resurrection? Are you patient and understanding of the importance of building relationships with others and the power of Fellowship? Fellowship is friendship it is comradery, it is, guess what, *Communion*!

I bet you are prepared to do many of these things, and you do not even realize it. The problem is, we simply have not done it before. Many believe that it is for our pastor or ministers to do. We have done an excellent job at inviting and bringing people to our church building and dropping them off with our pastor. LOL! Well guess what, that is not happening right about now, so, it is on you! You are the answer, and you already have everything you need on the inside of you. God lives on the inside of every believer. Chances are, you are likely the one they needed to hear from – perhaps God led them to you for just this reason.

I am just saying, it is already in you. Whatever area you feel you are lacking in, God will equip you with the knowledge, wisdom, and abilities so long as you go ahead and start! Find a scripture or two that are really personal for you, that caused you in a real way to give your life to Christ – share it with someone, share with them Romans 10:8-10, and this being the simplicity of inviting Christ into your life as Savior and the beginning of the process of making Him Lord. Be there to pray with them, love them, and answer what questions you can. – *Do not* be afraid to say you do not know the answer if you don't. There are many websites and other resources you can begin studying together. This is also a great question to ask of your leader, so that they can suggest some places for this type of foundational study online.

Whatever you do, don't leave them waiting without any assurance that they are loved by the Father – the assurance that right there in that moment, they can be saved. Don't leave anyone thinking they have to wait till the church building opens up again to receive salvation. No, let's not do that! Let's not leave them thinking they have to wait until the church building opens back up before you can take communion. Where is that found in the word of God? It is not. Grab that glass of water and cracker and together share Communion. It is a powerful form of fellowship with Jesus Christ and with one another.

If you have any questions or concerns at all regarding God or salvation, please don't hesitate to reach out to us at www.thearcinternational.org

and call us or submit your question on our contact form. We will reach out to you.

When you pray with someone, remember that prayer does not have to be long and drawn out. You do not have to speak in tongues. It's good if you do, but that is not a requirement for you to pray. Share the Word with them; You do not even have to know it by heart. Thank God for Bibles that can be accessed on our phones or tablets through apps, as well as on the Internet. You are saved, so you are a witness who has a testimony. Share it. Be prepared to befriend them; they may not be ready at that moment. Decide that you are going to be available to walk with them and let them know of your love for them regardless of where they are at that moment. We lift up Jesus before man, but God does the drawing! It worked 2,000 years ago, so you better believe it works today!

IT'S TIME TO GO YE!

I pray these spiritual, yet practical tips were helpful for you, and that a few of them made you chuckle. My prayer is that you are inspirited and now walk in the freedom to which Christ has made you free! You see, it is a problem if the "church ain't free." If we are not free, how will we introduce freedom in Christ to others? We cannot do it. It is time to be free.

Here are some Bible verses speaking about our freedom in Christ:

Galatians 4:4-7 – "But when the right time came, God sent his Son, born of a woman, subject to the law. God sent him to buy freedom for us who were slaves to the law, so that he could adopt us as his very own children. And because we are his children, God has sent the Spirit of his Son into our hearts, prompting us to call out, "Abba, Father." Now you are no longer a slave but God's own child. And since you are his child, God has made you his heir."

Romans 6:1-6 – "Well then, should we keep on sinning so that God can show us more and more of his wonderful grace? Of course not! Since we have died to sin, how can we continue to live in it? Or have you forgotten that when we were joined with Christ Jesus in baptism, we joined him in his death? For we died and were buried with Christ by baptism. And just as Christ was raised from the dead by the glorious power of the Father, now we also may live new lives. Since we have been united with him in his death, we will also be raised to life as he was. We know that our old sinful selves were crucified with Christ so that sin might lose its power in our lives. We are no longer slaves to sin."

Galatians 5:1 – "So Christ has truly set us free. Now make sure that you stay free, and don't get tied up again in slavery to the law."

It is time to experience the Father at levels we have not experienced Him at before. You can have the supernatural right here in your home where you are. Why? Because God is not confined to any one building, but He lives on the inside of us! So, wherever you are, He is there as well!

It is time to release old mindsets, routines, and habits and come fully into the knowledge and the presence of the Lord. I know doing things differently may take some getting used to. I know so many things are really challenging right now. I know that some of you all are saying "I'm not trying to fool with technology" to be a part of a larger gathering, but it may be all that you have right now. Even in that, do not forget the person that is sitting right next to you, or the neighbor across the street.

We don't know how long we will be under such health and safety restrictions, but either way, I have made a personal decision that I am *not* going to let anything stop me from experiencing the presence of the Lord alone and/ or in times of small group gatherings for prayer, teaching, and prophesy. I am not going to live without healing just because I do not have somebody in my house that can lay hands on me. I will lay hands on myself, because greater is He that is in me, than he that is in the world! I have all this on the inside of me, and so do you *if* you believe in God the Father, God the Son, and God the Holy Spirit. I will not waste what He sacrificed for me.

There are so many excuses or reasons that you can use to shut down now, but I am telling you, do not go out like that. All that God has done for you, all that He has been in your life, has shown *you* are powerful wherever you are. Being inside of the four walls of a church building does not increase the anointing on your life; it's just the opposite – it's when you set out to use the power inside of you, for the benefit of those who have not yet met that power – our God!

If you can prophesy in the church but not in your living room, or if you can prophesy in a church but not on your own doorstep, then that is a problem, because the Lord may send forth His Word at any time, and our boldness comes from Holy Spirit that's living on the inside of us, not from any other factor. We *must* keep moving forward. The world needs a touch from the Lord like never before. Apostle Betty Philips of Truth Ministries said this,

> *"We (us Christians) are so used to using our power on other power sources."*

In other words, we are so used to using the power of God that lives on the inside of us, in the church, and only for the benefit of other "church people."

In this season there is a great harvest of souls, that need to hear about Him through us, and that need to experience what has been locked up on the inside of us and inside the walls of the church building. It is time to let it all loose; it is time to come out from amongst that comfortable setting and go out into all the earth.

The Word tells us in Matthew 28:19:

> "Go ye therefore, and teach all nations, baptizing them in the name of the Father, and of the Son, and of the Holy Ghost: Teaching them to observe all things whatsoever I have commanded you: and, lo, I am with you always, even unto the end of the world. Amen."

It's Time to "Go Ye."

I love you all so much. Please consider sharing this book and/or the contents of it with family, friends, and even complete strangers! We must make some changes, and that will require us shifting a little bit, but we can do so in confidence. In Romans 8:38-39, the Apostle Paul tells us,

> "38 And I am convinced that nothing can ever separate us from God's love. Neither death nor life, neither angels nor demons,[b] neither our fears for today nor our worries about tomorrow—not even the powers of hell can separate us from God's love. 39 No power in the sky above or in the earth below—indeed, nothing in all creation will ever be able to separate us from the love of God that is revealed in Christ Jesus our Lord."

Thus, we cannot let the lack of a building or a large group setting separate us from the love God has for us, as well as the experiences of His supernatural presence, right? Let us release some of those things of old, so that we can experience the new and the *now* of God. Isaiah 43:19 says,

> "For I am about to do something new. See, I have already begun! Do you not see it? I will make a pathway through the wilderness. I will create rivers in the dry wasteland."

Moving Forward!

Someone once asked the question, "What is your Faith compelling you to do in this season?" I can honestly say that in this season my faith is compelling me to speak to the Church. My faith is compelling me to utilize all that is within me both spiritual and practical to be an aid to the church in this time of transition, to help the church unify and Move Forward!

Technology and the Internet must not be overlooked or shunned as methods of spreading the Gospel of Jesus Christ and connecting with others within our community and beyond. For many who have overlooked these tools because of their lack of knowledge, or because these tools have been misused by others - we must rethink this approach or perception. Our Pulpit has Move! In fact - I believe it's not just been moved, but it has been *Re-moved!* Where we can no longer hide behind it or exist on it as an island. We *must* engage, learn, and collaborate to keep moving forward. We must unify so that the Kingdom can expand, and the glory of God can permeate and heal the land.

This effort must be inclusive of an effort in our local churches to empower our congregants to use all that we have been pouring into them for years. No more "Pew members" as I often heard my grandmother say. The pews are gone! In essence, it's time to get-up-and-get out and use all that is in you both spiritual and practical to affect your families, your community, your cities, your nations, and your world! WE Are The CHURCH!

This is not and never has been a "one man show." It has always been an assignment for the Body of Christ, and every single member is needed, and every single gift and contribution is valuable.

Contrary to the belief of some, I do not see that the church has been shut down, but I see that the church has been released at a greater level into the Earth realm. I believe the Father has given us all 2020 Vision! And we can clearly see there is work for the Church to do – outside of the four walls. Truly, we are the answer – let's move forward together, let's use what we have to get the job done.

ABOUT THE AUTHOR

Victoria L. Burse

Victoria L. Burse is an ordained Pastor/Teacher, Leadership Catalyst, Mentor, Entrepreneur, and a prolific author. Victoria's heart for her Kingdom work is "That the man [man, women, child] of God may be competent, equipped for every good work" (2 Timothy 3:17).

As **Founder and Senior Pastor of the ARC International Ministries**, which is comprised of a Worship Center and a School for Christian leaders in the church and in the marketplace, Victoria teaches Biblical principles of leadership, personal development, and change. Near and dear to her heart are these ingredients she believes to be the keys to a prosperous life in every area, and the God-given recipe for growth and transformation.

Victoria holds a Master of Arts degree in Leadership from Luther Rice College and Seminary and has been honored for her ministry, leadership, and entrepreneurial accomplishments by the Sisters Empowerment Network of Atlanta and in the 2011 publication of *Who's Who in Black Atlanta*. She has consulted on numerous projects with organizations such as the U.S Department of Health and Human Services: Office of Community Service in Washington, D.C. and the Interdenominational Theological Center in Atlanta, GA. She also has had the honor of being a co-host on TV57's Atlanta Live Television Broadcast.

Residing in Stockbridge, Georgia, Pastor Victoria is married to Forest Burse (28 years) and together they are the co-owners of Front-Page Photography, (www.forestburse.com) a professional photography company that serves the states of Georgia and Mississippi by photographing weddings, special events, family portraits, and school pictures.

Experience the Ministry and the Message of God's Servant Teacher and Leadership Catalyst – Pastor Victoria L. Burse!

For Booking

E-mail: info@thearcinternational.org

Internet: www.victoriaburse.com

Phone: (678) 379-7652

Books

All available at www.thearcinternational.org

- ***Sabbath Songs*** – A Spiritual Coming of Age through the Transforming Presence of Jesus Christ (also available on Amazon.com)

- ***Destination Destiny*** – 12 Landmarks along the road to Destiny

- ***Who Moved My Pulpit? Who Moved My Pew?*** A Spiritual and Practical Guide for the Church on Embracing NOW and Moving FORWARD

I would love to connect with you socially!

Facebook:	facebook.com/victoria.burse
	facebook.com/theARCInternational
Websites:	www.thearcinternational.org
	www.victoriaburse.com
Instagram:	Pastorvictoria_thearc

BIBLIOGRAPHY AND RESOURCES

Johnson, Spencer, and Alexandria Library. *Who Moved My Cheese?: An Amazing Way to Deal with Change in Your Work and in Your Life*. Alexandria, Va., Alexandria Library, 2007.

Helpful Websites

"14 Church Statistics You Need To Know For 2020." *REACHRIGHT*, 2 Jan. 2020, reachrightstudios.com/church-statistics-2020/. Accessed 18 Aug. 2020.

"BIBLE VERSES FOR HOLY COMMUNION." *Www.Kingjamesbibleonline.Org*, www.kingjamesbibleonline.org/Bible-Verses-About-Holy-Communion/. Accessed 18 Aug. 2020.

Burse, Victoria. "Pastors Unity Fellowship." *The ARC International Ministries*, 2020, www.thearcinternational.org/pastors-unity-fellowship.html. Accessed 18 Aug. 2020.

"Do Pastors Feel Well-Equipped to Help Congregants Heal from Trauma?" *Barna Group*, www.barna.com/research/pastors-trauma-care/. Accessed 18 Aug. 2020.

"Five Trends Defining Americans' Relationship to Churches." *Barna Group*, 2020, www.barna.com/research/current-perceptions/. Accessed 18 Aug. 2020.

"Free Ministry Resources from Outreach!" *Go2020kits.Outreach.Com*, 2020, go2020kits.outreach.com/free-resources?utm_source=OP-Go2020-200521&utm_medium=email&maropost_id=713052128&mpweb=256-8884343-713052128. Accessed 18 Aug. 2020.

https://go2020kits.outreach.com/free-resources?utm_source=OP-Go2020-200521&utm_medium=email&maropost_id=713052128&mpweb=256-8884343-713052128

Jr, Ken Braddy. "5 Ways to Reach People Who Have Not Returned to Church." *Ken Braddy*, 3 Aug. 2020, kenbraddy.com/2020/08/03/5-ways-to-reach-people-who-have-not-returned-to-church/. Accessed 18 Aug. 2020.

https://kenbraddy.com/2020/08/03/5-ways-to-reach-people-who-have-not-returned-to-church/

Pastors Unity Fellowship. (2020). The ARC International Ministries. http://www.thearcinternational.org/pastors-unity-fellowship.html

the ARC. "House Church! How You Do That." YouTube, 25 July 2020, www.youtube.com/watch?v=ts1Wwf4Jb_o. Accessed 18 Aug. 2020.
https://www.youtube.com/watch?v=ts1Wwf4Jb_o

the ARC. "Hosting an Online Meeting with **ZOOM**." YouTube, 14 July 2020, youtu.be/5kxhvjiFCp8. Accessed 18 Aug. 2020.

https://www.youtube.com/watch?v=5kxhvjiFCp8&feature=youtu.be

Tomczak, Larry. "The Post Pandemic Church | ChurchGrowth.Org." *Church Growth*, 17 Apr. 2020, churchgrowth.org/the-post-pandemic-church/. Accessed 18 Aug. 2020.

https://churchgrowth.org/the-post-pandemic-church/

Help with Technology

"5 of the Best Church Online Giving Platforms." Outreach Blog, 5 June 2018, http://outreach.com/blog/best-church-online-giving-platforms/. Accessed 18 Aug. 2020.

"Church Giving: Mobile App, Online & Text Giving for Churches | Tithe.Ly." *Get.Tithe.Ly*, get.tithe.ly/. Accessed 18 Aug. 2020.

https://get.tithe.ly/

"Get Started Live Streaming - Computer - YouTube Help." *Support.Google.Com*, support.google.com/youtube/answer/2474026?hl=en. Accessed 18 Aug. 2020.

https://support.google.com/youtube/answer/2474026?hl=en

Haley, Bryan. "5 Rules For **Zoom** Newbies To Share With Your Staff." *ChurchLeaders*, 21 May 2020, churchleaders.com/ministry-tech-leaders/375797-zoom-newbies.html. Accessed 18 Aug. 2020.

https://churchleaders.com/ministry-tech-leaders/375797-zoom-newbies.html

"How to Use the Cash App For Your Business: A Complete Guide." *National Business Capital & Services*, 26 July 2019, http://www.national.biz/how-use-cash-app-your-business-complete-guide/. Accessed 18 Aug. 2020.

R., By, -, Ron Edmondsonhttp://www.ronedmondson.com/Ron Edmondson is a pastor and church leader passionate about planting churches, Edmondson, R., & Ron Edmondson is a pastor and church leader passionate about planting churches. (2020, July 31). **ZOOM** Meetings Are Here To Stay: Tips For Great Zooming. Retrieved August 18, 2020, from https://churchleaders.com/ministry-tech-leaders/379754-zoom-meetings.html

"Send Money, Pay Online or Set Up a Merchant Account - PayPal." http://www.paypal.com/, paypal.com. Accessed 18 Aug. 2020.

"StreamYard | Browser-Based Live Studio for Professionals." *Streamyard.Com*, 2020, streamyard.com. Accessed 18 Aug. 2020. https://streamyard.com

"The 7 Best Online Giving Companies For Churches." *REACHRIGHT*, 11 Apr. 2017, reachrightstudios.com/7-top-online-giving-companies-churches/. Accessed 18 Aug. 2020.

https://reachrightstudios.com/7-top-online-giving-companies-churches/

Thompson, Phil. "How to Livestream Your Church Service: A Practical Guide." *The Gospel Coalition*, 2020, www.thegospelcoalition.org/article/livestream-church-service-practical-guide/.

https://www.thegospelcoalition.org/article/livestream-church-service-practical-guide/

"Video Conferencing, Web Conferencing, Webinars, Screen Sharing." ***Zoom Video***, 2018, zoom.us/.

https://zoom.us/

Great Bible Study Sites/Apps

10 Best Bible Study Apps of 2020. (2020). Technical Explore. https://technicalexplore.com/best-bible-study-apps/

Bible.ORG. (2020). Bible.ORG. https://bible.org/

The Best Free Bible Study Apps For Busy Women. (2020). Graceful Abandon. https://www.gracefulabandon.com/bible-study-apps/

The International Bible Society. (2020). The International Bible Society. https://www.biblica.com/

www.ingramcontent.com/pod-product-compliance
Lightning Source LLC
Chambersburg PA
CBHW032011080426
42735CB00007B/570